Living Art

Orange Cup Coral

By: Cristina Kessler

*S*t. John in the U.S. Virgin Islands is so small most maps don't even show it. This tiny tropical paradise comprised of 16 square miles is a place where spiny green cacti meet the aquamarine sea; cobalt skies hug the distant horizon; huge humpback whales swim with tiny baitfish; and a rugged profile of forested mountains drop down to white sand beaches or rocky coastline.

The pristine state of the beaches and mountains of the island is no accident, for more than half of St. John is protected by Virgin Islands National Park. Development is limited to certain areas, while fortunately, Mother Nature owns the rest. Calm turquoise waters can transform into white-capped seas as quickly as blue skies turn black with menacing clouds. Hurricanes unleash their fury here, but in the end, the natural beauty always prevails.

I visited St. John for the first time in 1973. The sparkling greens and blues of the sea lapping against white sand beaches created a standard for every beach and island I visited over the next 30 years. Memories of the densely-forested mountains pitching down to the sea, stunning white stretches of sand, and the amazing colors of the water and the vibrant life below it, traveled the world with me. It was hard not to hold these mental pictures of Mother Nature's perfection on St. John as the standard that every other island, beach, cove or cay be judged by. Now these images are captured not only in my mind, but also vividly in print.

Living Art is a work of love by its creator, photographer Steve Simonsen. His emotional attachment to St. John shines through the superb photos he hopes will stimulate his readers to say, "Wow! How did I miss that?" Using a fresh eye on a familiar subject, he re-focused on the natural beauty of the island, capturing the colors and shapes, shadows and curves found on every coastline, mountain, and reef. Like a macro lens, he focused on the individual beauty of a single tree or the brightest fish, so often lost in the abundant bigger picture.

Driven by a vision, literally thousands of images were taken. In *Living Art* we see St. John from above and below, from close-up and from afar. For bird's-eye views Steve went aloft in a helicopter, and climbed to the highest points on the island. To record waterfalls and plant life he trudged deep into the thorny interior. The underwater shots of Mother Nature's creatures found him submerged, motionless, alongside the island's numerous colorful coral reefs. The photos in this book survived the scrutiny of a rigorous selection process, to showcase and share the best he has to offer of St. John. Whether zooming in on the subtle seasonal changes like shifting sands or schooling fish, the book's message is clear—slow down and see—rather than just look. Slow down and appreciate once again the beauty that is St. John.

There's something so very special about the island that it strikes up an immediate affinity with all those who experience it. Steve describes it best as, "What seeing a seahorse or swimming with a dolphin does to everyone—it's such a special experience, you just have to love it." The same can be said for *Living Art*, a pictorial collection vibrantly documenting what makes St. John one of the most special and beautiful places in the world.

Published in the United States Virgin Islands in 2003 by

Steve Simonsen Photography Inc.
P.O. Box 980
300-48 Great Cruz Bay Rd.
Cruz Bay, V.I. 00831 USA

ISBN: 0-9743166-0-1

Printed in China by Everbest

Designed by Cardinale Design

Cover photo: Cinnamon Beach

Dedication:

This book is dedicated to the memory of my brother Dale and his love of nature.

Friends of VIRGIN ISLANDS NATIONAL PARK

Part of the proceeds from the sale of this book will be
donated to Friends of Virgin Islands National Park

Poignant, timely, and stunningly beautiful, these images will only grow in importance as the years pass: eloquent and enduring testimony to a place that remains one of nature's masterworks.

Living Art

STEVE SIMONSEN

ST. JOHN USVI

Diary Creek

St. John

Great Tameshur Bay

Redband Parrotfish

Cinnamon Beach

Cruz Bay

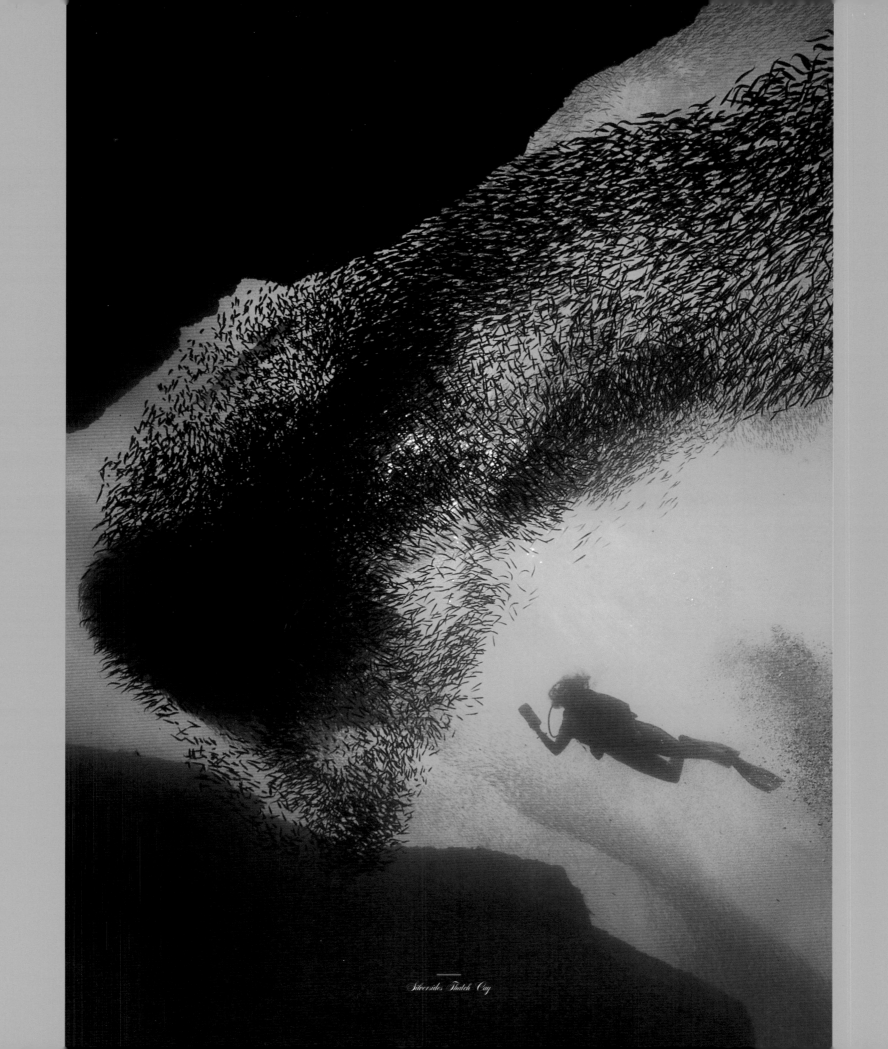

Silversides Thatch Cay

Johnson Bay

Ram Head

Christmas Tree Worm

Cinnamon Bay

Flamboyant Flower

20

Flamingo Tongue

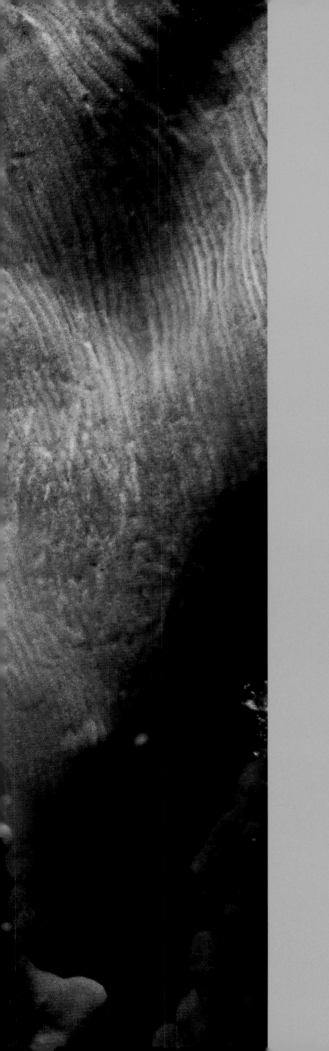

Coral Bay

Leinster Bay

Leinster Bay

Water Lettuce

Hurricane Hole

Turk's-head Cactus

Cinnamon Bay

Great Cruz Bay

Sensitive Plant

Coral Bay

Lured by the virginal abundance of undiscovered lands.

Hawksnest Bay

Enduring Eloquence
(A Brief Background of Historical Images of St. John)
By: David W. Knight, 2003

hrust from the ocean floor some ten million years ago by the violent collision of the earth's great shifting plates, the island of St. John is indeed one of nature's masterworks. As epochs passed, as the atmospheric tools of wind and water slowly transformed her jagged rock to soft rolling hills and verdant valleys, the island languished: nurtured only by the elements, devoid of human life.

We will never know who the first individual was to leave footprints in the soft coral sands of St. John, but in geological terms their arrival was a rather recent occurrence. It is believed that the island's earliest inhabitants migrated slowly up the Eastern Caribbean from the South American continent, arriving in the vicinity of the Virgin Islands roughly three thousand years ago. Lured by the virginal abundance of undiscovered lands, these Stone Age settlers were primarily hunter-gatherers that transiently occupied land along the island's watercourses and coastlines, moving on as readily available resources dwindled. While they had the ability to shape rudimentary tools from stone and shell, they do not appear to have possessed the skills to form clay into pottery. For this reason, the first human inhabitants of St. John are generally referred to as a Pre-ceramic people.

Pre-ceramic cultures remained a presence throughout the Virgin Islands for some one thousand years before their tenure was abruptly halted. Be it that they perished due to some disastrous natural occurrence, or were forced out, exterminated, or assimilated by a more dominant and sophisticated wave of immigrants, we simply do not know. We do know, that at a point roughly concurrent with the disappearance of the Pre-ceramic people, there appeared another population group distinguished by a more advanced material culture. These people also seem to have migrated along the island chain from South America, arriving in considerable numbers from about 200 BC. With them, they not only brought the ability to produce ceramic wares, but also a knowledge of agriculture. The fact that their culture was based upon the cultivation of the hardy manioc plant, from which they prepared a nutritious and durable staple food, meant that the Ceramic-period people tended to establish more permanent agrarian settlements. This afforded them the time and opportunity to advance themselves in areas not necessarily related to day-to-day foraging for sustenance: a fact displayed by the presence of detailed decorative adornments on their pottery and other personal, household, and ritualistic items.

So it is here, in the material remains left behind by successive Ceramic-period cultures that inhabited St. John for more than sixteen centuries, that we find humanity's first attempts to express the beauty and abundance of the island world that surrounded them. Ancient works of art formed from clay or carved in stone, wood, and bone, speak volumes of a time and place for which no volumes exist. An image, it is shown, is a most eloquent and enduring form of documentation.

With the encroachment of Europeans that began when ships from Christopher Columbus's fleet encountered the Virgin Islands in November of 1493, the era of an Amerindian presence on St. John rapidly drew to a close. While initial Spanish settlement efforts were concentrated on the larger more resource-rich islands of the Greater Antilles, little time had passed before the Spaniards began to venture out and actively extract the human and natural resources of the smaller islands such as St. John. It is believed that by 1520 nearly all of the indigenous peoples had either fled or been removed from the Virgin Islands.

Scant documentation exists relating to early European presence in the Virgin group; and as for images, our vision is clouded by the wildly distorted sea charts and equally crude elevation drawings of the period. It is known that Sebastian Cabot and Thomas Pert passed through the islands in 1517, but it was not until the emergence of growing numbers of European privateers into the West Indian theater near the close of the sixteenth century that the Virgins began to experience any significant increase in periodic visitation. In 1585 Sir Francis Drake explored the channel that now bears his name, and a decade later he again sailed along St. John's north coast with John Hawkins on their way to sack a Spanish treasure fleet in Puerto Rico. The Earl of Cumberland visited the Virgin Islands in 1597 and penned a rare descriptive account, portraying them as "...barren, craggy, and sandy, and wholly without inhabitants." In succeeding years any number of transient Spanish, French, Dutch, and British nationals ventured through the island chain, occasionally putting ashore in search of game, salt, fresh water, and log-wood, or to service their sea-weary vessels. Surely some of these individuals lingered for a time on St. John, but those that did left little-to-no evidence to speak of their presence.

And so for more than two centuries after Columbus's ships first sighted the Virgin archipelago, the island of St. John lapsed into a deep Márquezian solitude: often visited but formally unoccupied, a poor and remote relation amidst a family of increasingly wealthy West Indies sugar colonies. But then, in the spring of 1718, a small contingent of perspective settlers cautiously set out from the nearby island of St. Thomas and claimed St. John in the name of the Danish Crown. Within a decade, government and the systematic record keeping of events had been established. The island's long sleep had come to an end. St. John suddenly awoke to the ringing of tempered blades in her hardwood stands, the crackling flames of the clearers' fires, and the harsh realities of slavery and colonial domination.

By all accounts the early Danish-sanctioned settlers on St. John led a stark frontier existence, fraught with the elemental complexities of daily life. As the island's densely forested hinterland reluctantly gave way to human intervention, there was little tendency to pause and reflect on nature's beauty. It is no wonder then that there are few artistic renderings of St. John from this era. Among the earliest images to convey man's progress in taming the rugged topography of the island, is a German engraving of an overview of the Moravian and Dutch Reformed Church settlements on St. John's west side. Rendered from a sketch dating to approximately 1768, the print was published in an account of Moravian missions in the Danish West Indies by Christian G. A. Oldendorp in 1777.

But while depictions of its landscape in this period are limited, it is evident that large portions of St. John remained in a near natural state up until the great sugar-boom of the 1790s. As late as 1780, when Danish military engineer Peter Latharius Oxholm conducted the first general survey of St. John, he experienced considerable difficulty in negotiating the island's rugged terrain, apologetically writing the home government that "...had I completed the most accurate large-scale survey, a period of many months, perhaps years, would have been demanded as almost the whole land is still in bush." Despite the enormity of his task, Oxholm's resultant map of St. John stands out as a highly eloquent and enduring masterpiece of the cartographers' art. Upon its publication in 1800, the map provided the Danish public, and indeed the world, with a first enticing glimpse of the overall qualities and characteristics of Denmark's distant and exotic tropical colony.

The release of the first concise map of the island of St. John came at a point in time when the seeds of the Enlightenment had given root to the populist fervor of the nineteenth century. An era of great social, political, and ideological upheaval ensued; and in its wake, came new perspectives and a startling cultural awakening. Denmark entered its "Golden Age," in which her romantic and nationalistic youth set out with vigor to extol their country's virtues in literature, music, and art. Few individuals are as representative of this period as the gifted young naval officer and son of a former St. Thomas governor, Frederik von Scholten. During a trip to the Danish West Indies to visit his older brother (Governor-general Peter von Scholten), Frederik produced a series of pencil sketches and paintings of the islands. Among these works are three landscapes of St. John, all rendered in 1833: one, of the Carolina plantation and Coral Bay; another, of the island's broad interior valley with estates Susannaberg, Adrian, and Catherineberg; and, a sepia vignette of the waterfall and petroglyphs at Reef Bay. Although few in number, von Scholten's images are as important to the documentary record of St. John as any literary description of the time. Finally we can see with vivid clarity. After lingering for millenniums under a shroud of darkness, the island comes alive through the artist's hand, adeptly conveying the unique character of its landscape through the tools of color, composition, and light.

Throughout the remainder of the nineteenth century a succession of artists followed in Frederik von Scholten's footsteps, each contributing their individual styles and perspectives to our visual record of the island. Among the most notable was Reverend Henry Morton of Philadelphia, who visited St. John with his family in 1844. Over the course of his stay Morton executed a number of skillful drawings that include images of the Leinster, Caneel, and Carolina plantations, as well a panorama of Coral Harbor and a sketch of Turner Point on East End. In 1851, a young Dane, Fritz Melbye, undertook a brief excursion to St. John in company with his St. Thomas born friend and student Camille Pissarro. During the trip both artists are believed to have made sketches, but it was two renderings by Melbye, one of the Cruz Bay Battery and another of a provision grounds on Ajax Peak, that were to become the most recognizable and best loved images of St. John in this period. From an historical standpoint, however, it is a lesser-known work by Melbye that ranks among the most important depictions ever produced of the island. Painted from sketches made during his visit, Melbye's sweeping landscape portraying a mounted, white clad planter directing workers in a cane field, set against the lush backdrop of the Maho Bay Valley with the three stately great-houses of Wintberg, Mount Pleasant, and America Hill, stands out as a poignant parting image of the waning days of large-scale colonial agriculture on St. John. While the camera would make its first appearance on island within a generation, by the time it arrived there was only the rapidly diminishing vestiges of a plantation landscape for it to record.

With the near total collapse of St. John's sugar industry after the disastrous hurricane and earthquake year of 1867, the island once again lapsed into a long and brooding slumber. As the final decades of the nineteenth century droned on, the well sheltered port of neighboring St. Thomas emerged as a primary transit and refueling point for the increasing numbers of oceangoing passenger ships that now plied the world's waters. With this upsurge in regularly scheduled maritime traffic, came a corresponding rise in the number of transient visitors to the islands. The burgeoning age of tourism had inadvertently arrived, and with it came a sharp demand for small, easily transportable keepsakes. Soon, the streets of St. Thomas bustled with shops and emporiums competing for a share in the market of Panama hats, bay rum products, and photo souvenirs in the form of postcards, stereo-views, and photogravures.

Precisely when the first image of St. John was captured on camera remains unknown, but among the earliest photos that have been identified are a series of stereo-views of Cruz Bay dating from 1898. By the turn of the twentieth century, however, postcards and photo books with pictures of St. John had become less of a rarity, as the pioneers of Virgin Island photography, Dr. Charles Edward Taylor, his son, Clare Taylor, Edward Fraas, and Johannes Lightbourn, all began to produce and publish photographs of the island. Of these early photos, most are black and white images of cultural scenes, such as "native" households or activities like basket making and the manufacture of bay rum, but an occasional color-tinted landscape is not uncommon from the period. Still, it was not until after the purchase of the Danish West Indies by the United States in 1917, that the first concerted effort to document the entire island of St. John in photographs was carried out. At the request of the government of Denmark, in 1919 an architect by the name of Tyge Hvass arrived in the Virgin Islands on a mission to record the fading cultural legacy of the Danish colonial era. On foot and on horseback, Hvass and his party traveled throughout the islands of the former Danish West Indies, sketching architectural details, drawing plans of buildings and furniture, and taking photographs. Their efforts resulted in what is undoubtedly the single most comprehensive collection of photographic images up to that time period, and amongst them St. John is well represented.

It has been the better part of a century since Tyge Hvass traversed the dusty horse trails of St. John, and during that time countless photographs of the island have been taken. With the introduction of the first commercially available color film in the mid 1930s, the photographic record of St. John was instantly transformed from one of subtle tones and somber hues, to a celebration of vibrant color and the warm enveloping light of a tropical paradise. Since the creation of the National Park and the advent of large-scale tourism in the 1950s and 60s, parts of St. John have now become some of the most photographed places on the face of the earth. Yet amidst this flurry of snapshots, how many photographers have paused to consider the significance of their actions? For in every flick of a shutter, with each stolen instant, a unique and elusive image is captured.

With the publication of this unprecedented body of work, Steve Simonsen now joins the ranks of the most thoughtful and prolific documentarians in the history of St. John. Poignant, timely, and stunningly beautiful, these images will only grow in importance as the years pass: eloquent and enduring testimony to a place that remains one of nature's masterworks. ◎

It is evident that large portions of St. John remained in a near natural state up until the great sugar-boom of the 1790s.

Annaberg Ruins.

Waterlemon Bay

Leinster Bay

Reef Bay Creek

Tree Frog

Sunlight Underwater

Hurricane Hole

Great Cruz Bay

Coney

Little Cloudiness

Trunk Cay

Anole Lizard

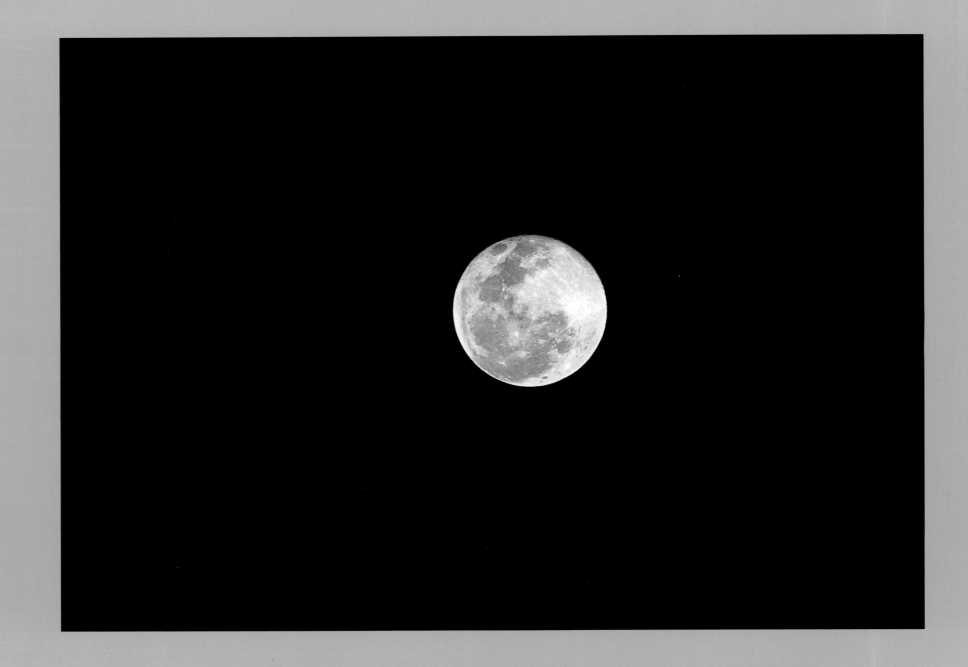

Full Moon

Caribbean Reef Squid

Gibney Beach

Hawksnest Bay

Trunk Bay

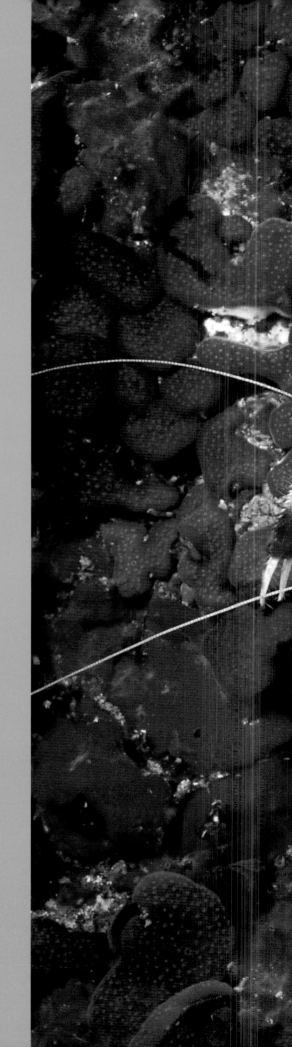

Banded Coral Shrimp

Cinnamon Bay

Carval Rock

Haho Bay

Queen Angelfish

Hurricane Hole

Southern Stingray

Petroglyphs.

Ram Hill

65

Susannaberg

Aurora

Lettuce Sea Slug

Reef Bay Valley

Maho Bay Gut

Sea Star

Frank Bay

Coral Bay

Redspotted Hawkfish

Cinnamon Bay

Francis Bay

Brown Booby

Booby Rock

Newfound Bay

Hummingbird

Queen Triggerfish

Cinnamon Bay

South Shore

Humpback Whale

Hermit Crab

Cinnamon Beach

Dilbij Peninsula

Milkweed

Silversides

Cumulonimbus.

Sea Stars

Maho Bay

Upper Reef Bay Waterfall

Denis Bay Ruins

Hawksbill Turtle

To me, the sea is like a person — like a child that I've known a long time. It sounds crazy, I know, but when I swim in the sea I talk to it. I never feel alone when I'm out there.

— Gertrude Ederle

One If By Sea

St. John

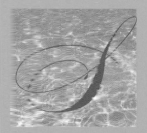

ome years ago I was returning to my home in St. John from a magazine assignment and found myself staring out the window at the island beneath me. I had been thinking about writing a book about St. John, a guide to its natural history showing it in all its glory from land, sea and air.

But to do that, I realized, I would have to snorkel and explore the entire shoreline. Suddenly, the idea of swimming all the way around St. John—photographing fish, sea life and topside scenic shots along the way—became a project unto itself.

I knew this needed some planning, so my first stop was the Virgin Islands National Park Visitor's Center in Cruz Bay, where I picked up an Army Corps of Engineers map. I discovered that the coast of St. John measures some 49 miles, including 51 bays and a few cay cays.

Next I developed a plan of attack. One of the beauties of St. John, but a logistical problem, is that many of its bays and beaches are in accessible from land. So even if I plotted an accessible beach where I could enter the water, it would be difficult at times to find a place where I could leave the water at the end of a day's snorkel journey. I did not look forward to hauling myself up on a rocky, wave-crashed beach, with all kinds of spiny sea urchins waiting to pierce my wetsuit.

After considering several options, I decided the best plan would be to drag my 14-foot inflatable boat behind me as I swam. The boat would provide me with access to every bay and cove along the way and give me a place to rest if I got tired. My safety back-up was the daily swim plan I filed with my wife Janet; she knew where I was swimming from and to, and when she could she would drive out to check on me.

Sometimes just getting started is the hardest part. People watching me pack my inflatable boat on my first day must have thought I was leaving for a month in the Arctic. But once I had all my gear aboard, I pointed her out to the east end of St. John. I had decided to do the hard part first by bypassing the tourist-favored and lovely north shore bays at Hawksnest, Trunk, Cinnamon, Maho, Francis and Leinster.

The east part of St. John is on the windward side of the island, and the usual strong wind creates big waves that pound on the jagged and rocky shore. It is no wonder that this part of the island is virtually inaccessible by land. Most people wouldn't venture out here even if they could.

After more than two hours of being tossed around in the rough water, I began to feel sick and climbed back into my boat, moving into a quieter bay. Over a sandwich and a beer I began a reflection on this thing—one bay down, 50 to go, and what was I doing?

A few weeks later, I returned to the northeast shore on a much nicer and calmer day. I was able to cover almost three miles from East End Point to Brown Bay. It was a glorious day for swimming and free-diving, and I photographed the large and healthy undisturbed reefs on the wilderness side of St. John.

Pastel-colored parrotfish, a huge nurse shark too quick for my shutter finger, a turtle, and schools of blue tangs patrolled amidst the gardens of sea fans. The wind and tides pushed me gently along past Newfound, Haulover, and Mennebeck Bays, and I found some of the finest snorkeling I had yet seen on the island. ∎

THE MAGNIFICENT SEVEN OF NORTH SHORE

Eventually, on my months-long project to circum-snorkelate the island, I hit these seven bays, most of them well-known to snorkelers.

Leinster Bay is home to Waterlemon Cay, surrounded by clear, calm water, colorful sponges and large sea stars. It's the most reliable spot for turtle sightings on St. John. It's also one of the nicest snorkel spots on the island, and I spent hours here exposing frame after frame.

At Mary Point, my wife dropped me in the water with my cameras and planned to meet me at Maho Bay and its roadside beach. I perfected my "St. John Olympic Snorkel Crawl" during this stretch along a shoreline made up of an interesting mix of marine plants, rocks and coral reef. I saw an octopus stretched out on a rock as if sunbathing. I tried sneaking up on some floating pelicans and managed to swim alongside a turtle, which let me get some great shots.

Cinnamon Bay is the longest, widest and sometimes windiest beach on St. John. The snorkeling is good along the rocky end of the beach (to the right, facing the water). The reef here is an ancient one, with coral colonies that have cemented together over the eons in a series of overhangs, ledges and cave-like crevices. It's a long swim out to Cinnamon Cay, but worth every stroke to see the abundance of soft corals, sergeant majors, and gray and French angelfish that inhabit the cay's waters.

Famous Trunk Bay is a gorgeous sandy beach lined with palm trees and a small inviting cay near the shore. Here the Park Service has sunken underwater signs to create a snorkel trail. In summer, Trunk Cay is surrounded with dark clouds of fry fish, and patrols of large silvery-scaled tarpon cruised in and out of the thick congregation of fry. Stingrays glided over the sandy shallow bottom. Trunk Bay is an occasional nesting site for turtles and within 30 minutes I spotted three of them swimming along the healthy coral formations east of the cay.

Between Trunk and Jumbie Bays is a very popular reef full of schools of blue tangs, doctorfish and surgeonfish, elkhorn coral, sea fans and the occasional nurse shark.

I spent hours in Hawksnest Bay snorkeling the three distinct coral reefs separated by sandy channels that run out from the shore. There were damselfish, porcupinefish, squid, peacock flounder, and brain and elkhorn coral. To the west side of Hawksnest, at the rocky point that's part of the Caneel Bay Resort, I found a dramatic, action-packed reef. I also found some tricky currents near the point, and an increase in boat traffic—be forewarned.

Picture-perfect Honeymoon Beach is one of seven beaches on the Caneel property. This beautiful spot is visited frequently by day-sailors and can also be accessed by hiking trails from Cruz Bay. Swimming along the shallow reef between Honeymoon and Solomon, I was trailed by needlefish and houndfish. ∎

SOUTH SHORE

As I swam into Rendezvous Bay, the water was calm and I could see squid everywhere. I glanced up at the beautiful homes that dot the hillside, looking down on Rendezvous' large bay, awash in gorgeous shades of blue and aqua. I wondered if they could tell that below the magnificent colors is mainly just sand and turtle grass.

Past Boatman Point I encountered an amazingly dense school of baitfish. The sky above me was suddenly busy with bird traffic. Brown pelicans, boobies and laughing gulls dive-bombed for lunch. Moments later, two large tarpon cruised silently by no more than five feet away, a startling sight given their shark-like profile.

Inside Hart Bay, the protection from the ocean swells was gone and suddenly my attention was drawn from fish and reef to the problem of trying to keep my boat from pulling me onto the rocky shore. The waves caused the tether around my waist to jerk me up and down, and finally I just climbed aboard and fired-up the engine to escape the dangerous surf.

Two days later I was dropped off at Hart Bay without the boat to try to make a long, four-mile leg to Great Cruz Bay. Unhindered, but also a little apprehensive, I struggled out of Hart Bay. Suddenly the swells were behind me and with the pushing effect of wind and waves, I made it all the way to Great Cruz Bay in under an hour. I swam carefully across the opening of the bay checking for boats, and as I approached Moorehead Point, I felt the currents behind me. This, combined with the clear water beneath me, told me that the tide was coming in and conditions were favorable for me to continue all the way to Cruz Bay—a big chunk of real estate on my itinerary.

Along the way, I stopped in Turner Bay, where the reef yielded a large number of colorful queen angelfish and a rare batfish in the sand. In all my years diving around the Virgin Islands, the only other batfish I've ever seen was beneath the pier in Frederickston on St. Croix. Of course, this was one of the few days that I didn't lug my cameras along. I was triumphant as I rounded Gallows Point and headed straight into Cruz Bay. I had covered over four miles in less than two hours. ■

CORAL BAY

With my cooler packed with goodies and my spirits high, I headed to explore Coral Bay. This is one of St. John's largest and most convoluted harbors, deep enough and protected enough that it was once considered for a U.S. Navy base.

Deep inside is Hurricane Hole, which still provides a safe anchorage for boats during a storm. The red mangrove trees and eerie calm water shelter a nursery

for barracuda and grunt, butterflyfish, octopuses, crabs, silversides, and many others including the upsidedown jellyfish. It's a sci-fi snorkel spot, but due to its fragile ecosystem, it's probably best if reserved for only the best snorkelers.

There is a little rocky reef in Long Bay (one of the many little coves within Coral Bay) that forms a small ledge running parallel to the shore. I spotted a series of rocks jutting out of the water called Pelican Rocks on the charts. Other snorkelers arrived by the beach, and soon there were about 10 of us diving and snorkeling around the rocks. It's a good spot. We saw healthy star coral, needlefish, queen and gray angelfish, damselfish, colorful Spanish hogfish, and the usual turtle or two. I finished my visit by swimming through Round Bay, where the dolphin sequences for the movie "The Big Blue" were filmed.

One of the best-kept secrets on St. John is Reef Bay. Usually the waters are choppy in the tradewinds, and it can be accessed only by boat or hiking trails. But during the winter, when storms in the North Atlantic throw powerful swells against the north shore, places like Reef Bay, Lameshur Bay and Salt Pond are usually quiet and peaceful.

When I told people I was planning to swim around Ram Head, they all said, "Wait for a calm day." Normally wind and waves make this corner of the island especially treacherous. As I finished swimming the other parts of the island, I began checking the weather conditions each day for that unusual calm day. As the weeks crawled past, I knew it had to be done before the onset of the seasonal "Christmas Winds".

Early one morning, my head still ringing from a Christmas party the night before, I stumbled out of bed at 4:45 am and checked the weather. Winds were reported as being light, from the east at only 6 mph. This might be it!

I headed for Ram Point before sunrise, dreading the stretch of shore I had put off until last. I was in the water at 6:50 am and swimming full speed ahead for Coral Bay before the effects of my morning coffee wore off.

In the first 25 minutes, I saw three eagle rays, and two turtles, banged through the tough surf and found myself surrounded by schools of the fish I had been photographing all summer. I took it as an omen, a signal from the deep that despite cracked fins, blistered toes, tedium and tiredness; I was in the home stretch.

Four hours later, near Fortsberg, in Coral Bay, I heaved myself up into my boat for the last time. Mission accomplished. I could lay claim to being the first and only person to swim all the way around St. John.

Maybe I was just overly waterlogged, but I swear I could hear the fish below me slapping their tails in applause. ■

Now I could lay claim to being the first and only person to swim all the way around St. John.

—Steve Simonser

Rendezvous Bay

Genti Bay

South Shore

Fungi Passage

Durloe Cays

Reef Bay

Humpback Whales

Gibney Beach

Hennebeck Bay

Annaberg Ruins

Lightning

Ripples and Ray

Mangrove Anemone

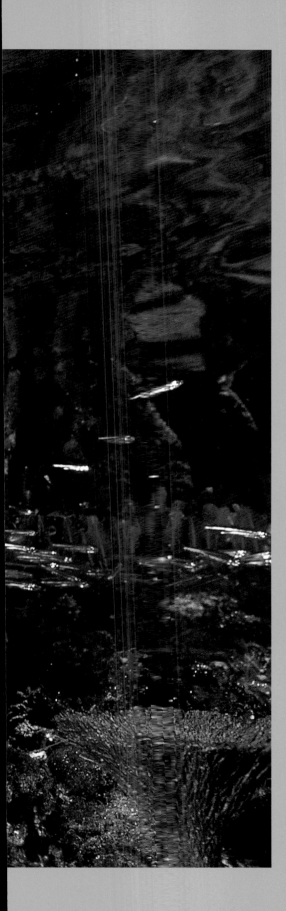

Congo Cay

Bordeaux Mountain

Rendezvous Bay

Trunk Bay

Trunk Bay Beach

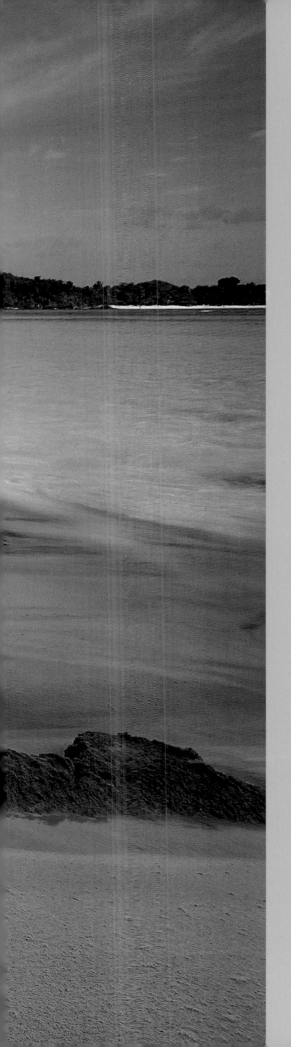

Cruz Bay

Salt Pond

Reef Scenic

East End

123

Privateer Bay

Francis Bay

Cocoloba Cay

Carolina Ruins

Katydid

Cinnamon Bay

Schooling Sonnets

Pelican Rock

White Point

Teinder Bay

Ixora

Please Point

Tarpon

Coral Bay

Hydrothermal Rock

Great Cruz Bay

Fairy Basslet

Steven Cay

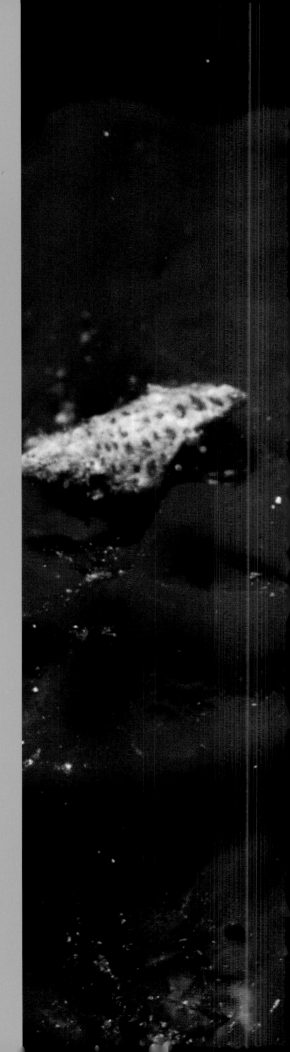

Solomon Beach

Lettuce Sea Slug

Wash Rocks

Whistling Cay

Princess Creek

Bottlenose Dolphin

Cabrillo Horn Point

Flanagan Island

Solomon Beach

Francis Bay

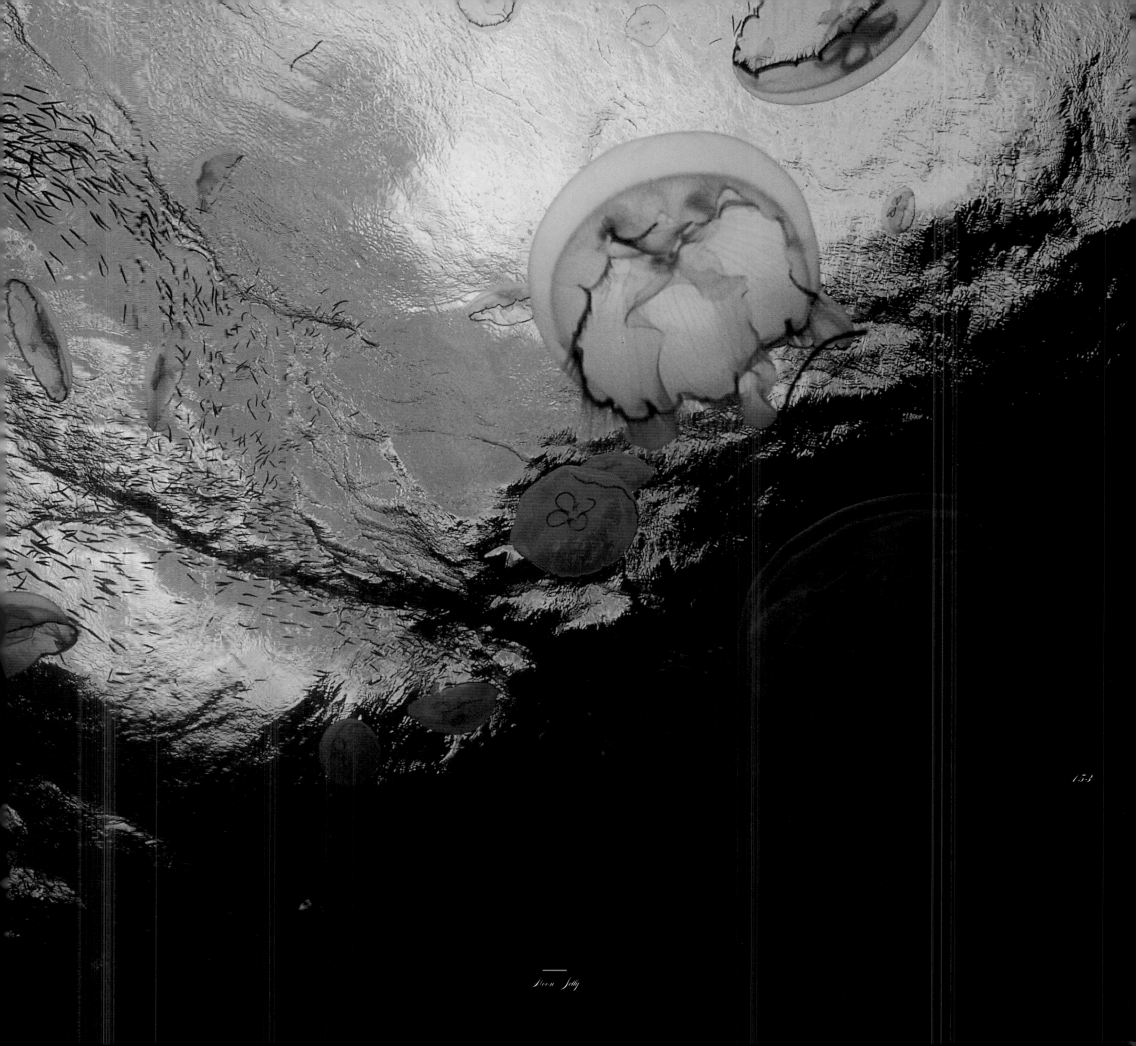

Moon Jelly

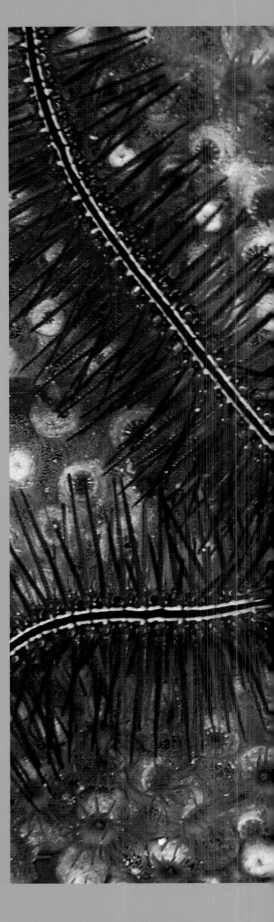

Bordeaux Mountain

Sponge Brittle Star

Pillsbury Sound

Reef Scene

Reef Bay Creek

Hawksnest Bay

St. John

Silversides

Kiddel Bay

Salt Pond Bay

Ram Head

Zebra Butterfly

Reef Bay

Reef Scene

Long-Horn Nudibranch

Cancel Bay

Hurricane Hole

Cinnamon Beach

Red Night Shrimp

Round Bay

Hawksnest Night

Haulover Bay

Dittlif Point

Trunk Bay

Hahe Beach

Coral Bay

Henley Cay

Peppermint Goby

Maho Beach

Johnsons Reef

Francis Bay

South Shore

Red Mangrove

Whistling Cay

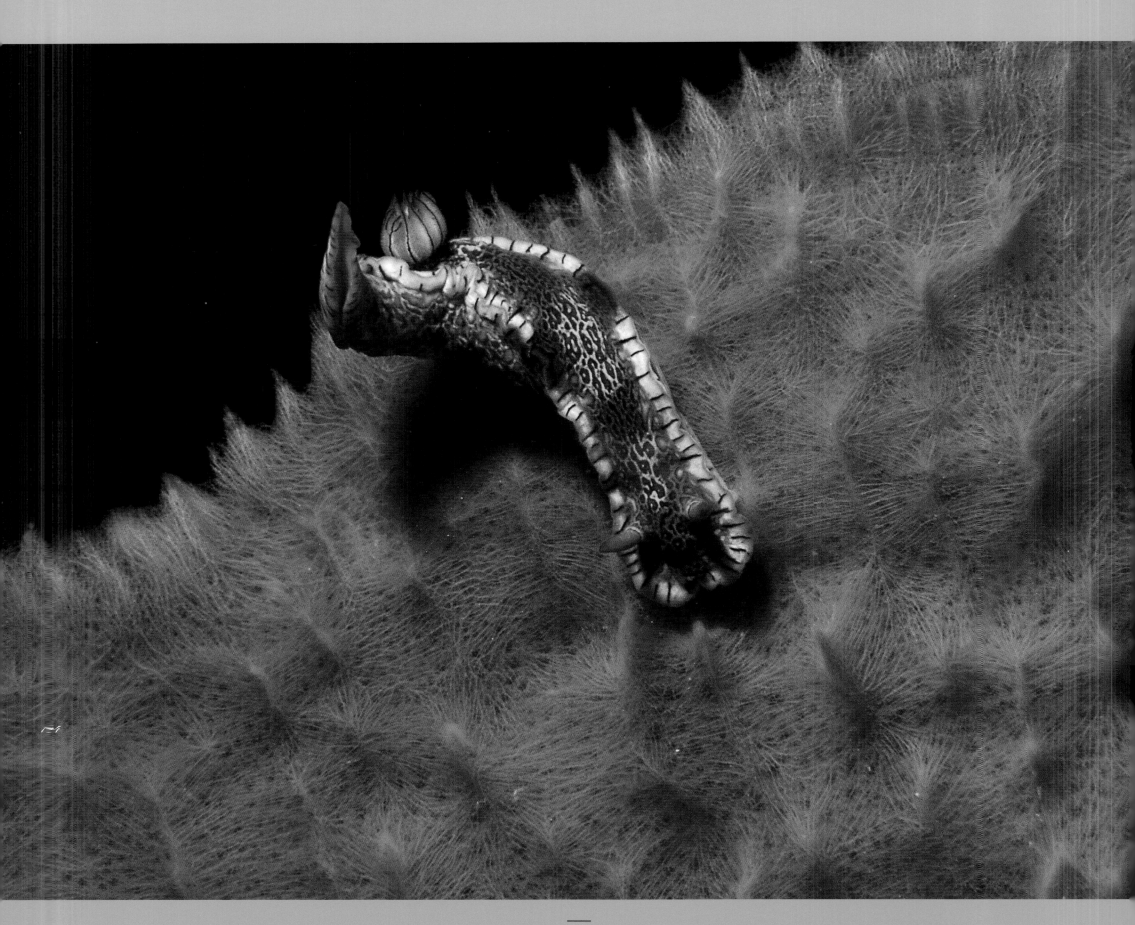

Nudibranch

195

66 The Reef Bay Valley lies between Bordeaux Mountain and Camelberg, Peak.

67 On the other side of the road from the Reef Bay trailhead is a gut that spills out at Maho Bay.

68 A cushion sea star in Borek Creek.

69 Trunk Bay from the east, looking west.

70 Sunrise over Coral Bay, Round Bay and Norman Island.

71 The redspotted hawkfish has red and golden spots on its head and tassels on the tips of its dorsal spines. They are the only member of the hawkfish family in the Atlantic.

72 Beach sands are sculpted by wind and water. Generally beaches erode during winter storms and are built back up by long periods of calmer seas in summer. A dead tree stands as evidence to beach erosion at Cinnamon Bay.

73 View of Francis Bay and Mary Point from the overlook.

74 Boobies are commonly seen diving on schools of baitfish or silversides. This one seemed unafraid as I approached it from beneath, out in the vicinity of Frenchcap Cay.

75 Booby Rock out from Salt Pond Bay offers great diving and is a nesting site for roseate terns, mountain doves, ground doves, bridled terns and laughing gulls. Boobies have not been observed there since 1975.

76 Newfound Bay near the eastern end is a small, intimate bay with good diving and snorkeling.

77 Antillean crested hummingbirds are commonly seen in the wild as well as around gardens and feeders.

78 The queen triggerfish is locally known as "old wife".

79 View of Cinnamon and Francis Bays from Lizard Hill.

80 The south shore including Rendezvous, Fish, Reef, Europa and Little Lameshur Bays.

81 A humpback whale calf breaching out from Turner Bay.

82 A hermit crab in a West Indian top shell.

83 A view of Cinnamon Beach, Peter Bay and Cinnamon Cay.

84 The view southwest from Dittlif Peninsula includes Frenchcap Cay, Dog Rocks and Dog Island.

85 Giant milkweed.

86 There are about 10 different species of small silver, fork-tailed schooling, fish, that when grouped together, are virtually impossible to distinguish underwater. Therefore, they are all referred to as silversides or baitfish.

87 Cumulonimbus rain clouds cause sudden downpours that can be seen coming, from quite a distance. Generally the rain does not last very long.

88 Leinster Bay is not only home to many cushion sea stars, but also some of the finest snorkeling around St. John.

89 A view of Francis and Maho Bays.

90 Above the lower falls there is a larger one seldom visited. It's worth the scramble under brush and over loose rocks to see.

91 The Denis Bay ruins.

92 A hawksbill turtle at night near Little St. James.

94 An aerial perspective of St. John from above Two Brothers, Pillsbury Sound.

97 Dawn over Dittlif Point and Rendezvous Bay.

98 Deep inside of Reef Bay is Genti Bay.

99 The convoluted south shore showing Reef Bay, Europa Bay, Little Lameshur Bay, Great Lameshur Bay, Grootpan Bay, Kiddel Bay, and Salt Pond Bay.

100 View of Whistling, Cay, the Fungi Passage, Little and Big Tobago and Mary Point.

101 Durloe Cays consist of Rata, Ramgoat and Henley. St. John is in the distance.

102 The small Indian mongoose was intentionally introduced to the Caribbean in 1872 to help control the rat population in the sugar fields.

103 The beach at the west end of Reef Bay.

104 A humpback whale cow and her calf in Pillsbury Sound.

105 A split-level view of Gibney Beach.

106 An aerial view of Mennebeck Bay, Princess Bay, Mardenboro Point, Brown Bay and Mary Point.

107 Annaberg, is the setting for living history demonstrations of sugar cane growing, the baking of traditional breads, and basket weaving.

108 The turpentine tree is also called "gumbo limbo". Another common name is the "tourist tree" because the bark is red and always peeling.

109 Two tributaries feed the Fish Bay Gut.

110 A thunderstorm produces lightning bolts that strike the sea, temporarily blocking out the view of St. Thomas from Great Cruz Bay.

111 A southern stingray glides over the sun dappled ocean floor. Rays inhabit sandy areas and often lie motionless on the bottom, covered with sand.

112 Close to the surface in Borek Creek a mangrove anemone and a small group of split-crown feather dusters co-exist along, with green grape algae and flat-top bristle brush, commonly referred to as "shaving brush algae".

113 Dense groves of teyer palms are present on Thatch and Congo Cays, as well as at Mary Point, Bordeaux Mountain and elsewhere on St. John.

114 Largely undisturbed, Bordeaux Mountain and Reef Bay Valley are prime habitat for wild boars that feed primarily on roots.

115 Coral reefs, sand, and seagrass beds combine with shadows from passing clouds to create a display of brilliant blues and greens in Rendezvous Bay.

116 Trunk Bay from the overlook.

117 The terrain on St. John ranges from dry, cactus-covered cliffs and salt ponds on the eastern end at Privateer Bay to the moist subtropical forest of the northwestern slopes.

118 Algae-covered rocks on the eastern end of Hawksnest Beach.

119 Serene St. John, the least developed of the U.S. Virgin Islands, is a quiet wonder of nature. The capital town of Cruz Bay is affectionately dubbed "Love City".

120 Wind-whipped waves cause a foamy whitish froth along the leeward side of the salt pond at Salt Pond Bay.

121 The best diving and snorkeling spots are not along the shoreline of the island, but rather around any of the surrounding cays. Out of reach from the destructive forces of winter storms a deep, fringing, reef flourishes along the south side of Mingo Cay.

122 An aerial of the eastern-most tip of the island showing Privateer Bay, East End Bay, and Newfound Bay.

123 Sunrise over Privateer Bay.

124 Moonset from Francis Bay includes Carval Rock, Outer Brass Hans Lollick and Little Hans Lollick, the latter of which are islands north of St. Thomas.

125 *Cocoloba uvifera* is the Latin name for sea grape. Cocoloba Cay is located just east of the mouth of Fish Bay.

126 The Carolina ruins are found in the middle of a creek bed at the base of Bordeaux Mountain and probably served as a cistern to hold water.

127 A katydid on a bromeliad.

128 Cinnamon Bay is where you'll find the longest, widest and windiest beach on the north shore.

129 Southern sennets are in the barracuda family, but only grow to 13" long. They form loosely polarized schools and will occasionally circle a diver.

Hermit Crab

Creating the book "Living Art", was a labor of love. A number of individuals and organizations have helped make this book possible and I am incredibly grateful. I would like to thank my lovely wife, Janet and my son Jesse for their unending support and encouragement. The very talented Kathy Cardinale for her creative design work, David Knight for his scholarly historical account and Cristina Kessler for her beautiful introduction. I would also like to thank Ann Marie Estes and Bob Shinners of Low Key Watersports for their support throughout the years. I would especially like to thank Maggie Day and Joe Kessler along with Friends of Virgin Islands National Park for their involvement. And a special thanks goes out to the entire staff of the National Park Service.